PHOTOGRAPHS BY

HAROLD LLOYD

EDITED BY

SUZANNE LLOYD HAYES

3-D Hollywood

SIMON & SCHUSTER

NEW YORK LONDON TORONTO SYDNEY TOKYO SINGAPORE

SIMON & SCHUSTER
SIMON & SCHUSTER BUILDING
ROCKEFELLER CENTER
1230 AVENUE OF THE AMERICAS
NEW YORK, NEW YORK 10020

DESIGNED BY KAROLINA HARRIS
MANUFACTURED IN THE UNITED STATES OF AMERICA

1 3 5 7 9 10 8 6 4 2

LIBRARY OF CONGRESS CATALOGING-IN-PUBLICATION DATA
LLOYD, HAROLD, 1893–1971.
3-D HOLLYWOOD / PHOTOGRAPHS BY HAROLD LLOYD ; EDITED BY SUZANNE LLOYD HAYES.
P. CM.
1. MOTION PICTURE ACTORS AND ACTRESSES—CALIFORNIA—LOS ANGELES—PORTRAITS. 2. CELEBRITIES—
CALIFORNIA—LOS ANGELES—PORTRAITS. 3. HOLLYWOOD (LOS ANGELES, CALIF.)—SOCIAL LIFE AND CUSTOMS—
PICTORIAL WORKS. 4. PHOTOGRAPHY, STEREOSCOPIC. I. HAYES, SUZANNE LLOYD. II. TITLE.
PN2285.L56 1992   92-14385 CIP
ISBN 0-671-76948-0

ACKNOWLEDGMENTS

I would like to thank the following people for their help and inspiration:

Jean Picker Firstenberg

Brian Martin

Roy Brooks

Peter Langs

Richard Correll

Gloria Lloyd Roberts

Jeffrey Hayes

J. William Hayes

Nancy Gates Hayes

Daniel Strone

Bob Bender

Virginia Clark

Roddy McDowell

David Hume Kennerly

FOR MY SON, CHRISTOPHER,
AND DAUGHTER, JACQUELINE,
WHO ARE THE JOYS OF MY LIFE

—WITH LOVE, **SLH**

HAROLD LLOYD

Harold Lloyd was one of the giant stars of the silent era in Hollywood. As a film comedian he ranked with Chaplin and Keaton.

Lloyd was born in Nebraska in 1893. He moved to California with his family and began in Hollywood after touring as an actor with a stock company. He worked with Mack Sennett and then with Hal Roach, developing his famous screen character, the typical American boy, with his trademark horn-rimmed glasses. Among Lloyd's best-known films are *Safety Last, The Freshman, The Kid Brother,* and *Speedy.*

At the peak of his success in the 1920s, Lloyd began to build his estate, Greenacres, one of the most splendid residences in California. The forty-four-room Italian Renaissance mansion was situated on sixteen acres in Beverly Hills. It was beautifully landscaped, with formal gardens, a cascading waterfall, an Olympic-sized swimming pool, and a nine-hole golf course.

Lloyd began taking 3-D photographs—using a process then known as stereo photography—in the 1940s. He was the first president of the Hollywood Stereoscopic Society, whose other members included Dick Powell, Art Linkletter, Ronald Colman, and Edgar Bergen.

Harold Lloyd died in 1971 at the age of seventy-seven.

FOREWORD

Harold Lloyd loved life. There was no greater testament to this than the magnificent Christmas tree that stood year-round in the Sun Room at his sixteen-acre estate in Beverly Hills called Greenacres. I've always felt fortunate that I was raised by a man who thought every day was Christmas.

I arrived at Greenacres as a baby and lived there until Harold's death in March of 1971. I called him Daddy, and to me he will always be just that—the man who loved me, the man who cared for me, the man who introduced me to the most exciting world any child could hope to experience, a fantasy world seen through the eyes of Harold Lloyd. The centerpiece of the estate was an opulent forty-four-room Italian Renaissance mansion surrounded by formal Rose Gardens, Cascade Gardens, and an Olympic-sized swimming pool. Guests would drive up a one-and-a-half-mile-long driveway past a nine-hole golf course (Jack Warner was our neighbor and had the back nine on his estate), and if they had children, they would drop them off to play in the Playhouse, a life-sized dollhouse that had running water, electricity, and pony stables. The Playhouse had been built for my mother, Gloria, and I spent many happy hours there, creating my own fantasies.

My grandfather's film career had ended long before I was born. This meant that he had a lot more time to spend with me than he had had for my mother, her sister, Peggy, and her brother, Harold Jr., who grew up while their father was in the spotlight during the 1920s and '30s. As a matter of fact, until he took me to a screening of one of his films at the Cannes Film Festival, I thought Daddy was a photographer. He pursued many interests during his later years, including painting, magic, bowling, and handball. But in the years that I lived with him, photography was his passion. He felt the challenge of trying to capture that perfect moment in light, shape, and form that all photographers strive to preserve. He was always experimenting with a new kind of film, state-of-the-art meters, new lenses, or different lighting setups. The estate was his proving ground, and I was always asked to stand here, find the light there, tilt my head up. When I played the temperamental model, he'd go to the kennels on the estate and drag out one of the seven Great Danes that he raised to act as my stand-in. Those poor dogs—I'm sure they never forgave me! He also took pictures of his friends, who were constantly visiting the estate for tennis and swimming parties. If you were a friend of Harold Lloyd's, you had better not mind having your picture taken! I didn't realize it at the time, but a lot of these visitors were famous actors, directors, writers, and politicians.

Harold traveled the world in style and traveled it often. I was lucky enough to take my first of many trips abroad at the tender age of three! We would take the Super Chief train across the country and then board the *Liberté* for the Atlantic crossing to Southhampton, England. It was on these trips that Daddy became the most fanatical of shutterbugs! He loved shooting interesting people from all walks of life and composing panoramic shots of beautiful places. He took some of his most spectacular 3-D photos on these trips. I'll never forget him sitting in his den and getting the biggest kick out of looking at our travel photos, which through a viewer look as if you can reach right into them. I must admit, though, that there were times when his obsession with getting the perfect picture got on my nerves. I know it drove my grandmother, Mimi, crazy! He scared us to death when he climbed to the top of the Golden Gate Bridge or when he went out on top of the Space Needle in Seattle. He was totally fearless with a camera. And taking a car trip through Europe with him was a unique experience. We used to call him "Stop the Car Harry!" because that's what he was always telling the driver to do. Whether in a small country village or in the middle of the Champs-Elysées, if he saw something he thought would make a great picture, he'd be out and gone. Sometimes he would leave us for hours while he went exploring down a country lane or waited for the right light on a hilltop. We'd wait in the car or sit in a café, or we might be told to just go on and he'd find a way to catch up.

I was always curious and interested in what he was doing and would sit with him for hours on end while he edited his photos in his studio. After his death when we catalogued all his 3-D photos, the count well exceeded three hundred thousand. Most of these had been mounted into 3-D frames by his secretary, Roy Brooks, who started with him back in the twenties and lived at the estate for forty years. Roy always loaded all the film cartridges and then sent them on ahead to each destination on our itinerary. He had to load a lot of film because each shot in Daddy's 3-D camera, a Stereo Realist, required two exposures.

The last few trips we took to Europe together, I went along more as a photographer's assistant than as a granddaughter. Daddy taught me how to load the cameras, check the meters, and take readings. He shot much faster if he had several cameras ready to go at the same time, so I was always busy. I also carried his camera bags, which guaranteed I wouldn't gain any weight on the trip!

Daddy was the first president of the Hollywood Stereoscopic Society, formed in 1950; other charter members included Dick Powell, Art Linkletter, Ronald Colman, and Edgar Bergen. Then, in the years just prior to his death, Daddy spent a great deal of time with a second group of friends who specialized in 3-D photography. They called themselves the Happy Seven and traveled throughout the country shooting pictures and putting on shows called "The Magic Carpet" for the Photography Society of America.

So I grew up living and traveling with an intensely creative man who had a true love affair with film. Long before I was born, he made movies that he not only starred in but produced. In his films he was very particular about camera angles and was the first person to use the false perspective of distance and height to create the most spectacular stunt sequences seen in the early films of Hollywood. He was a true innovator and pioneer. When he retired from making movies I think it was only natural that he turned to photography to continue to satisfy his love for the medium of film and his passion for life.

When my grandfather passed away at Greenacres, I was by his side. He had lived such a full life it was hard for him to believe it was over. But he wanted to make sure that people down through the years would benefit from his legacy and left me to oversee and administer a film and memorabilia trust. He also created a foundation so that Greenacres could be preserved as a public museum and park. I tried to run that museum for three and a half years, but the city of Beverly Hills made it too difficult and the house had to be sold at public auction in 1975. It has since become an historical site, which prevents the house from being torn down or removed. Unfortunately, the beautiful grounds around the house have been subdivided and developed. The proceeds from the sale went to benefit movie preservation and set up scholarship funds for film students across the country. And in Harold's honor I had a soundstage built at the University of Southern California.

For the past few years I have been working on rescoring and preserving all of my grandfather's films. I also produced a documentary, *Harold Lloyd: The Third Genius,* with film historians Kevin Brownlow and David Gill, for Thames Television. It aired as part of the PBS "American Masters" series and was nominated for an Emmy in 1990. When I was working in the film vaults and going through Daddy's memorabilia, I ran across hundreds and hundreds of boxes of his slides. As I looked at them, they gave me such pleasure that I thought it would be wonderful to publish them so that everyone could see them. I was fortunate to have the help of my friend Brian Martin, but it still took me five months to catalogue and organize Daddy's slides. A lot of the photographs brought back a flood of memories, and although at times it was difficult, it was always pleasurable. We were constantly surprised by the people, places, and things that "Stop the Car Harry!" had shot. I hope that everyone who looks at this book will enjoy seeing the world through the eyes of Harold Lloyd. I know I did.

SUZANNE LLOYD HAYES
Beverly Hills, California
January 1992

Harold Lloyd's photography room at Greenacres, cluttered with cameras, lights, gadgets, and thousand of slides. Daddy called it his "Chaos Room."

Self-portrait of Harold Lloyd in his photography studio at Greenacres, which he had converted from a handball court when he no longer played the game.

Stars at Greenacres

Charles "Buddy" Rogers in the Poplar Garden at Greenacres, early 1950s. Rogers's wife, Mary Pickford, was god-mother to Harold Jr.

Publicity shots of Dorothy Provine taken at Greenacres, for her role as Pinky Pinkham in the television series, "The Roaring Twenties" (1960–62).

Carol Lynley as a starlet in a photo shoot at Greenacres, early 1960s.

Marilyn Monroe came to Greenacres for a publicity shoot. Here she is poolside, wearing the same outfit she modeled in *How to Marry a Millionaire* (1953). Gloria Lloyd remembers that Marilyn kept saying, over and over, "I hate careless men," a line that was recorded. In the estate's Olympic-sized pool, Johnny Weissmuller had taught Gloria, Peggy, and Harold Jr. to swim.

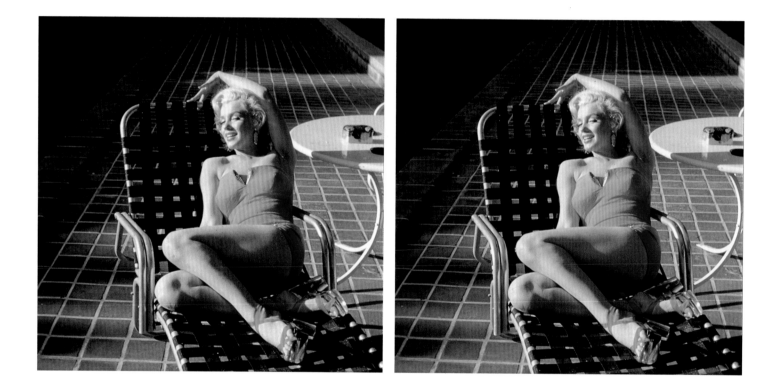

Marilyn by the kennel area on the way to the pool.

Greenacres

Hallway leading to the Formal Dining Room. The Music Room is to the right, and to the left is the Center Courtyard. The sixteenth-century tapestry on the wall once belonged to the King of Belgium; it was a gift to Daddy and Mimi, my grandmother, from Douglas Fairbanks and Mary Pickford, for their first wedding anniversary on February 10, 1924.

The Sun Room, or Orangery, off the landing to the Formal Dining Room. Before it became home to the Christmas tree, it was used as a party room, with French doors on three sides leading to the Rose Garden, Center Courtyard, and sweeping back lawn. The room was hand painted with flowers and plants indigenous to California.

The Cascade Gardens, copied from the Villa d'Este in Italy. The landscape artist, A. E. Hanson, was sent to Europe twice to lay out the plans for Greenacres. This fountain could reach a spray height of 25 feet, and the overflow was recycled to the waterfall that dropped 120 feet to the canoe run and golf course below.

Rear view of the estate, with the Poplar Garden in the forefront and the stairs to the left leading to the back lawn.

View of the Poplar Garden from the edge of the Rose Garden. The tennis court is directly behind the gazebo. Both sides of the garden are lined with cypress trees.

Daddy and me in front of the Christmas tree at Greenacres, about 1956. The decorations on the tree became more elaborate each year, until finally the tree was left up year-round. The last tree Daddy put up, in 1967, had over 8,000 ornaments.

Daddy and me on the *Liberté* in 1955, crossing from New York to Southampton, England—my first of many transatlantic crossings. Mimi refused to fly.

Tab Hunter (center, rear), Harold Jr. (right), and Ann Blyth (far right), 1950s. The others are unidentified.

Tab Hunter and friend. Tab was a good friend of the family. Mimi had met him in art class; he had been painting purple

horses.

Gossip columnist Hedda Hopper, famous for her hats, chats with Harold Lloyd at the wedding reception of Lloyd's daughter, Gloria Lloyd (my mother) to William Guasti at Greenacres, September 16, 1950 (rival columnist Louella Parsons also attended; it was rare indeed for the two to appear anywhere together).

Hollywood Candids

The night before Philippe Halsman's landmark 1952 photo session with twenty-five-year-old Marilyn Monroe for *Life* magazine, he visited his friend Harold Lloyd to see his collection of 3-D photos. The next day, Lloyd went with Halsman to Marilyn's apartment in Los Angeles, which was modest but full of books —including the works of Hemingway, Tolstoy, Einstein, and Flaubert—evidence of her intellectual curiosity. Halsman's April 7, 1952, cover for *Life* drew the attention that Marilyn needed to help turn her from starlet to star.

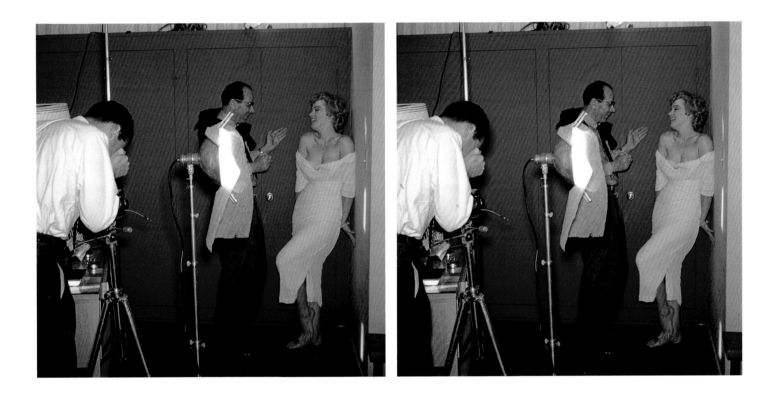

Philippe Halsman chats with Marilyn to relax her, as his assistant focuses the camera.

Shots similar to Halsman's black-and-whites for *Life*.

Just visible on the table is a photo of the great Italian stage actress Eleonora Duse, an inspiration for Marilyn.

Jayne Mansfield posing at a meeting of the Hollywood Stereoscopic Society at Romanoff's restaurant in Beverly Hills, about 1953. Harold Lloyd was one of the founding members of the 3-D club.

Jayne Mansfield being photographed by 3-D club member Bob Cummings, star of the television series "Love That Bob" (1955–59), in which he played a playboy photographer.

Art Linkletter and showgirls from Shipstad and Johnson's *Ice Follies* show at a meeting of the 3-D club, 1955.

Candice Bergen as May Queen at Westlake School for Girls, Holmby Hills, 1964. I was a fourth-grader there at the time, participating in the event, and Daddy was there taking pictures like a good Daddy.

Candice Bergen, the future Murphy Brown of the television series. Her father, Edgar Bergen, was active in the 3-D camera club.

Hollywood at Play

Gymnasts at Santa Monica's "Muscle Beach," 1950s. Harold Lloyd's beach house was nearby, and he would just take off with his camera and enjoy shooting the sights.

At the Los Angeles Open Golf Tournament, Riviera Country Club, Pacific Palisades, circa 1952–53:

Alan Ladd, about the time he made the classic Western *Shane.*

Sterling Holloway. A good family friend who was also active in the 3-D club. Sterling was the voice of Winnie-the-Pooh, and the narrator of *Peter and the Wolf* in Disney's animated films.

At the Los Angeles Tennis Club, 1950s. The Lloyds were great tennis fans:

Mickey Rooney and Peggy Lloyd in the family box. Mickey was a good friend of Peggy and Gloria's.

Humphrey Bogart and Lauren Bacall.

Hollywood
Behind the Scenes

From right to left: Producer Howard Hughes, director/writer Preston Sturges, and actress Frances Ramsden take a break at Sturges's restaurant, The Players, during the filming of Harold Lloyd's last film, *The Sin of Harold Diddlebock* (1947). The film was about what had happened to Lloyd's screen character since the 1920s; its opening football sequence is from Lloyd's popular 1925 film, *The Freshman*.

Preston Sturges.

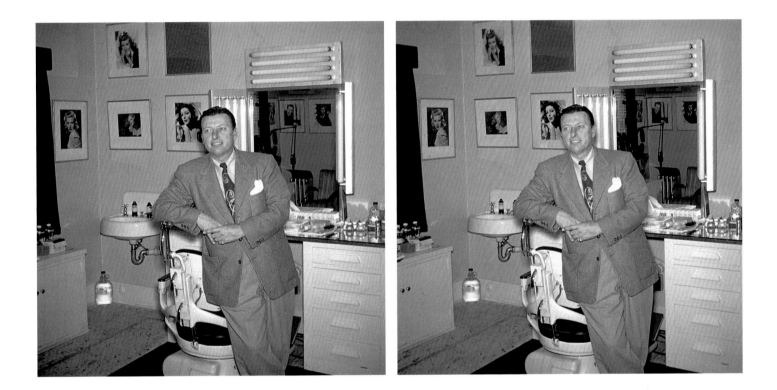

Wally Westmore, head of makeup at Paramount for thirty-five years, in his studio. A close family friend, he and his wife Edwina always joined the Lloyds at holiday dinners. The Westmore brothers—Wally, Perc, Bud, and Frank—were all in the makeup business at the top studios and formed a real Hollywood dynasty.

Dick Powell as a Mountie in *Mrs. Mike* (1949). He was another friend of the family, as well as vice-president of the 3-D camera club.

Glenn Ford braves the Alps in *The White Tower* (1950). A friend of Harold Lloyd's, he dated Peggy Lloyd at one time.

Tyrone Power as a Mountie, staving off an Indian war in *Pony Soldier* (1952). A good friend of Lloyd's, Ty often came to the house for lunch and to work on scenes.

Richard Burton was nominated for an Oscar for his performance as a centurion in *The Robe* (1953), the first Cinema-Scope feature.

Harold Lloyd and Bob Hope on a movie set, early 1950s. Good friends, and two great comedians from different eras.

Parades and Ceremonies

SHRINERS

Daddy was very active in the Shriners and their charitable activities. Over 100,000 people attended the "Electric Pageant" in June 1950 at the Los Angeles Coliseum, which was held in honor of Harold Lloyd, who was Imperial Potentate at the time. The following photos were taken at that event:

Roy Rogers.

Roy Rogers on Trigger.

Red Skelton in his Shriners robe.

Arlene Dahl.

Gary Cooper.

George Murphy, the actor who would later become a U.S. senator.

Ronald Reagan, president of the Screen Actors Guild at the time.

Harold Lloyd at the Grand Canyon, 1950, when he was traveling for the Shriners as Imperial Potentate. This photo was taken by his secretary, Roy Brooks.

General Douglas MacArthur is given a hero's welcome in San Francisco upon his return from the Korean War in 1951:

Addressing the crowd from the podium.

In his car.

Riding in the parade.

William Boyd as Hopalong Cassidy, with his horse, Topper, made regular appearances in the Rose Parade in Pasadena. Here they are in the 1950s.

Richard and Pat Nixon riding in the Rose Parade, 1953. Nixon was the parade's grand marshal and had just been elected vice-president of the United States.

Dwight and Mamie Eisenhower at the Rose Bowl, early 1960s. Harold Lloyd was good friends with Ike and had been the head of the California delegation at the 1952 Republican Convention in California, where Ike was nominated for president.

At the George Eastman Award Dinner, Rochester, New York, on November 19, 1955. Standing, left to right: George Raft, Maurice Chevalier, Ramon Navarro. Seated, left to right: Lillian Gish, Gloria Swanson, Mary Pickford, Janet Gaynor.

At the dinner after the taping of the "This Is Your Life" television show, hosted by Ralph Edwards, in honor of Harold Lloyd. Chasen's restaurant, Los Angeles, December 14, 1955:

Clockwise: Ralph Edwards (standing), Hal Roach, Mildred (Mimi) Lloyd. Sterling Holloway, Wally and Edwina Westmore, and Lucille Roach also attended the dinner.

Prints of Harold Lloyd's hands, feet, and trademark eyeglasses preserved at Grauman's Chinese Theatre, Hollywood, November 21, 1927.